18
PRINCIPLES OF
Manhood

For Young Males

John Bolden
Bolden Publishing

18 Principles of Manhood for Young Males

John Bolden

18 Principles of Manhood for Young Males

Bolden Publishing
P.O. Box 2025
Kalamazoo, MI 49003
Copyright © 2020 by Bolden Publishing
All Rights Reserved. Reproduction of text in whole or in part without the written consent by author is not permitted and is unlawful according to the 1976 United States Copyright Act.

All scriptural quotations are taken from *Biblegateway.com*, www.biblegateway.com. Accessed Sept. & Oct. 2020.

Sources for word definitions:
Dictionary.com. www.dictionary.com/.
Merriam-Webster. www.merriam-webster.com/.

"48 Famous Failures Who Will Inspire You To Achieve." *Wanderlust Worker*, www.wanderlustworker.com/48-famous-failures-who-will-inspire-you-to-achieve/.

Cover design and book production by:
Bolden Publishing
Cover illustration is protected by the 1976 United States Copyright Act.
Copyright © 2020 Bolden Publishing
Printed in the United States of America

John Bolden

I dedicate this book to my father, Joseph Bolden, Jr. He taught me the power of knowing who you are & he continues to teach me what makes a man great.

18 Principles of Manhood for Young Males

Table of Contents

Introduction 2
How To Control Your Anger 5
Your Thoughts 7
Conquering Fear 8
Your Thoughts 10
Avoiding Temptation 12
Your Thoughts 14
Overcoming Lust 16
Your Thoughts 18
Don't Be Lazy 20
Your Thoughts 22
Effective Communication 23
Your Thoughts 24
Being A Responsible Man 26
Your Thoughts 28
Acknowledge Hidden Pain 30
Your Thoughts 31
The Importance of Forgiveness 33
Your Thoughts 34
Dealing with Failure 35
Your Thoughts 37

Identity	39
Your Thoughts	42
Be Teachable	44
Your Thoughts	46
Accept Correction	48
Your Thoughts	50
Accountability	52
Your Thoughts	53
The Importance of Good Character	55
Your Thoughts	57
The Role of a Father	58
Your Thoughts	60
Keep Growing	62
Your Thoughts	64
Build A Relationship with God	66
Your Thoughts	69
PRAYERS	71

18 Principles of Manhood for Young Males

Introduction

Growing up, I was very inquisitive. I can remember seeking help from my father and the men around me to understand *me*. I needed answers. I wanted to understand my thoughts, perspective, and emotions. I longed for a resource that was transparent. My son is the same way, and I created the *18 Principles of Manhood for Young Males* for him and any young male that is looking for a resource on how to navigate through their journey of manhood.

The journey to manhood requires transparency and guidance. In the *18 Principles of Manhood for Young Males*, we will confront many of the issues and internal battles that young males face. We will examine and discuss the foundational characteristics needed to become men of character and integrity.

No matter your age, the goal of this resource is to give you language for your future. The important questions to ask mentors and teachers that you can learn from. The words and skills to express your emotions in a healthy way. The wisdom and instructions that can save you from making mistakes and learning the hard way.

As young men, it is important to have a solid foundation to stand on. The challenges that you face are complex but not impossible. A lack of guidance has caused many young males to spiral out of control on a path towards destruction. Young males are being counted out and expected to fail. But I believe otherwise. I believe God has a purpose, plan, and destiny for all young males.

John Bolden

Declaration

I want you to read the sentence below out loud…

I am ready to create change in my life that will prepare me for manhood.

John Bolden

How To Control Your Anger
Principle #1

Anger – A strong feeling of annoyance, displeasure, or hostility.

Ephesians 4:26 (NIV) states, *"In your anger do not sin": Do not let the sun go down while you are still angry."*

Anger is an emotion that we all feel at some point in our lives. As young males, it is important that you learn how to properly deal with anger. It is unhealthy and dangerous to allow yourself to be angry for long periods of time. It is also vital to pinpoint the source of your anger. Ask yourself the following questions: Why am I so angry all the time? Who or what causes me to be angry? How do I behave when I get angry?

When left unresolved, anger can lead to detrimental actions such as violence, arguments, or even self-harm.

Violence

Violence is the expression of a deeper issue that has not been resolved. Childhood trauma such as witnessing or experiencing domestic violence or other forms of abuse can be a source of anger and violence. Unchecked anger and outbursts of violence can lead to abusing loved ones, harming animals, or even being destructive at home or in school. Unprocessed anger has driven many young men to juvenile centers and prisons for murder, rape, domestic violence, and other violent crimes.

18 Principles of Manhood for Young Males

Arguments

When you are angry, you may struggle to communicate effectively and find yourself yelling or arguing a lot. Arguing can keep you agitated and on edge causing anger to build up. It is important to be mindful of triggers. Is it the tone that someone speaks to you in? One way to be proactive in this area is taking a moment to pause and gather your thoughts before speaking.

Self-Harm

Anger, rage, and other emotions that are not expressed out loud can be turned inward. Cutting, substance abuse, hitting your head on hard surfaces, flesh burning, and other harmful behaviors are acts of self-harm. Self-harm is often a way of escape from the emotions, thoughts, and feelings that need to be expressed and processed.

The inability to control your anger can have a negative impact on every aspect of your life from employment to relationships. One bad decision can cause a ripple effect that may take months or years to recover from. Learning to talk your frustrations out is important. Speaking with a counselor or mentor are helpful ways to process suppressed anger. Also, participating in helpful activities, hobbies, and connecting with friends are effective coping methods.

Focus Scripture:

Hot tempers start fights; a calm, cool spirit keeps the peace.
(Proverbs 15:18 MSG)

John Bolden

Your Thoughts

Conquering Fear
Principle #2

Fear – A distressing emotion aroused by impending danger, evil, pain, etc., whether the threat is real or imagined; the feeling or condition of being afraid.

Fear is a silent killer. It paralyzes its victims in a way that keeps them from progressing in many areas of life. Fear will cause you to miss opportunities and not live life to the fullest. It can manifest in different ways such as fear of the dark, fear of rejection, fear of the unknown, fear of failure and so forth. But you must understand that it is not God's will for you to live your life full of fear.

When a person is dealing with fear it has a way of crippling their life in one way or another. Fear can cause you to avoid relationships, marriage, parenting, or any type of responsibility. Fear can even cause you to become emotionally impaired to the point that you are unable to function properly. Allowing fear to settle in your heart will affect the way you think and behave.

I can remember classmates in middle school and high school that did not apply themselves at all because they feared rejection from our peers. Do not allow today's fear to hinder your growth as a man.

II Timothy 1:7 (AMP) says, *"For God did not give us a spirit of timidity or cowardice or fear, but [He has given us a spirit] of power and of love and of sound judgment and personal discipline [abilities that result in a calm, well-*

balanced mind and self-control]." The statement 'fear not' appears 365 times in the Bible. One time for every day of the year! Conquering fear requires changing your mindset. Study and learn from the actions of someone that you admire. For example, my son for a short period of time, was afraid of dogs. But after watching me confidently interact with dogs he let go of his fear.

Overcoming fear sometimes means being vulnerable. Being open and honest, putting your feelings out there without worrying about the response. Take a leap of faith! It is important to express out loud what you are thinking or desire to communicate.

Prayer and positive confessions are effective techniques of conquering fear. Words have power! Reading, thinking, and speaking encouraging words throughout your day will reset your mind and help you become confident in the areas that you are fearful in.

Focus Scripture:

The Lord is my light and my salvation; Whom shall I fear? The Lord is the strength of my life; Of whom shall I be afraid? (Psalm 27:1 NKJV)

Your Thoughts

Do not follow the crowd. Let the crowd follow you. Be a leader.

Avoiding Temptation
Principle #3

Temptation – the act of tempting or the state of being tempted especially to evil.

All males, at some point in their lives, will deal with temptation. James 1:13-15 explains in detail that it is because of our own lust that we are tempted. Remember, you are not the first or the last – *every* man gets tempted. The good thing is that whenever temptation comes GOD ALWAYS MAKES A WAY OF ESCAPE! Temptation will come but you do not have to give in to it.

Temptation comes in many forms such as quick money schemes, sex prior and outside of marriage, acts of violence, stealing and so forth. When temptation arises, you must consider the consequences. How much are you willing to pay? Fast money may seem easy but twenty years in prison is not. A one-night stand may not seem like a big deal but consider all the potential outcomes and you will see why you must make the right choice.

It is important to pay attention to how your body reacts in certain situations. An increase in your body temperature or feelings of nervousness can be signals of temptation. Being aware of the signals can help you make the right decisions in the moment. It is important to build your will power to say "no" *in the moment*. Implementing prayer and scripture memorization will be vital to your growth in this area.

Being accountable to someone will help you when you are feeling weak. Do you have someone in your life that can talk you through those moments? Remember, the journey to manhood requires transparency so being honest about your struggles is important.

Focus Scriptures:

No temptation [regardless of its source] has overtaken or enticed you that is not common to human experience [nor is any temptation unusual or beyond human resistance]; but God is faithful [to His word—He is compassionate and trustworthy], and He will not let you be tempted beyond your ability [to resist], but along with the temptation He [has in the past and is now and] will [always] provide the way out as well, so that you will be able to endure it [without yielding, and will overcome temptation with joy]. (I Corinthians 10:13 AMP)

Let no one say when he is tempted, "I am being tempted by God" [for temptation does not originate from God, but from our own flaws]; for God cannot be tempted by [what is] evil, and He Himself tempts no one. 14 But each one is tempted when he is dragged away, enticed and baited [to commit sin] by his own [worldly] desire (lust, passion). 15 Then when the illicit desire has conceived, it gives birth to sin; and when sin has run its course, it gives birth to death. (James 1:13-15 AMP)

Your Thoughts

John Bolden

Be accountable to someone!

Overcoming Lust
Principle #4

Lust – to have a yearning or desire; have a strong or excessive craving, very strong sexual desire.

You cannot allow lust to consume you as a young male. This is a major issue that has plagued man since the beginning of time. God's word states the following:

- I John 2:16 (NLT): *"For the world offers only a craving for physical pleasure, a craving for everything we see, and pride in our achievements and possessions. These are not from the Father, but are from this world."*
- Romans 6:12 (AMPC): *"Let not sin therefore rule as king in your mortal (short-lived, perishable) bodies, to make you yield to its cravings and be subject to its lusts and evil passions."*

Be mindful of the type of music that you listen to and what you are viewing on TV. Certain websites, videos, and social media can be detrimental to your growth as a man. You must consider the consequences and potential long term affects if what you watch or listen to only promotes sinful choices such as sex before marriage, drug use, alcohol abuse, etc.

As a young male, you may find that it is a struggle to read the Bible. But within the scriptures you will find help and instructions to deal with lust and sexual sin. Psalm 119:11 (ESV) says, *"I have stored up your word in my heart, that I might not sin against you."* Seek wisdom from the Word of God in a translation that you can understand such as *The*

Message (MSG) or the *New International Version* (NIV). The Bible, while thousands of years old, has answers for what you face in your life. It is a vital and trusted resource!

It is also important that you are connected to a church and community that can help you understand the Word of God. Attending church on a regular basis is important so that you can hear a credible pastor teach and break down the scriptures. YouVersion's *The Bible App* is a great resource for focused Bible study plans. Christian books devoted to the topic of overcoming lust can also help you grow and maintain discipline in this area.

Focus Scripture:

I will set nothing wicked before my eyes…It shall not cling to me. (Psalm 101:3 NKJV)

Your Thoughts

John Bolden

A man that does not work should not eat. Real men work.

Don't Be Lazy
Principle #5

Laziness – the quality of being unwilling to work or use energy, idleness.

"If a man don't work, he don't eat!" This is a familiar saying that originated from a passage in the Bible.

II Thessalonians 3:10-13 (MSG) says, *"Don't you remember the rule we had when we lived with you? "If you don't work, you don't eat." And now we're getting reports that a bunch of lazy good-for-nothings are taking advantage of you. This must not be tolerated. We command them to get to work immediately—no excuses, no arguments—and earn their own keep. Friends, don't slack off in doing your duty."*

In Luke chapter 5, we see Jesus demonstrate the power of obedience as it relates to work. He called a few of the disciples while they were wrapping up a long, unproductive day out on the lake. Their obedience to Him resulted in a boat sinking, net breaking, life changing catch. All 3 disciples left everything that day to follow Him.

God cannot guide you to an abundant life if you are lazy. Laziness results in you wanting much but having very little. Nothing in life comes without hard work and effort on your part. You must get out of bed and be motivated to win!

Entitlement is a form of laziness. Things do not just come to you. A strong work ethic gets you the job or your own successful business. Laziness starts in your mind and it shows in your body language. It also shows in your behavior. Not being on time, not being a man of your word, and sleeping too much are all signs that laziness is present.

During those days when you have no drive, no focus, and no motivation, focus on *your* "why." A lot of men acknowledge that they would be further along in life if they had not wasted time. Laziness can mean you have access to everything you need to succeed but lack the motivation to put it into action. Stop sitting around feeling sorry for yourself and get up and do something. God has a plan for your life and the world is waiting on you!

Focus Scriptures:

The soul of a lazy man desires, and has nothing; But the soul of the diligent shall be made rich. (Proverbs 13:4 NKJV)

Some people dig a fork into the pie but are too lazy to raise it to their mouth. (Proverbs 19:24 MSG)

Your Thoughts

John Bolden

Effective Communication
Principle #6

Communication – The imparting or interchange of thoughts, opinions, or information by speech, writing, or signs.

As a young male, you must learn how to communicate your thoughts. The inability to effectively communicate and express yourself can lead to frustration. When you feel stressed out and your emotions start running high you may misread or misinterpret communication from those around you.

Men sometimes have a hard time communicating when it comes to *deep hearted* issues. Poor communication skills can often be traced back to childhood trauma. Take the time now to learn how to thoroughly convey your thoughts and opinions. Bottling up all your emotions and never expressing them is not healthy. Honest and clear communication will be crucial in relationships as you mature. Technology, for this principle, can be a great teacher. There are tons of videos on YouTube, podcasts, and blogs that can teach you how to develop your communication skills.

Focus Scriptures:

Let your speech always be gracious, seasoned with salt, so that you may know how you ought to answer each person. (Colossians 4:6 ESV)

The tongue has the power of life and death, and those who love it will eat its fruit. (Proverbs 18:21 NIV)

Your Thoughts

Are your friends influencing you or are you influencing them?

18 Principles of Manhood for Young Males

Being A Responsible Man
Principle #7

With adulthood comes responsibility. It is impossible to be successful as an adult and not shoulder any responsibility. There is also no way around responsibility as it pertains to manhood. Being a responsible man includes managing finances, maintaining employment, effective leadership of your family & home, active parenting, and being a loving spouse to your wife.

Balance

Balance is defined as an even distribution of weight enabling someone or something to remain upright and steady. I have seen quite a few young males that were not properly prepared for manhood and they buckled under pressure. This causes some young men to give up and abandon their responsibilities.

It is important to learn skills as a young man to balance school, work, family time, and other aspects of life. Balance is the ability to prioritize and manage different aspects of your life in a productive way. Having balance does not mean you are doing everything equally. It means you are focused on your obligations and managing your time effectively.

As you transition into manhood, you can learn how to prioritize all aspects of your life with the help of God. As Proverbs 13:22 (KJV) says, "*A good man leaveth an inheritance to his children's children…*" A good man seeks wisdom and knowledge, always keeping God first and consistently working to build a legacy for his family. Proper time management and realistic priorities will help you maintain order and discipline throughout your life. Get organized. Create a plan. Set a schedule. Remain consistent.

Focus Scripture:

But seek first the kingdom of God and his righteousness, and all these things will be added to you. (Matthew 6:33 NIV)

… Your Thoughts

John Bolden

Making a wise decision is not always the popular thing to do.

Acknowledge Hidden Pain
Principle #8

Pain – 1. physical suffering or distress, as due to injury, illness, etc. 2. mental or emotional suffering or torment.

Hidden – concealed; obscure; covert.

Acknowledging hidden pain refers to exposing any secrets or suppressed trauma that has happened in your life. Processing your feelings about events or issues from your childhood is a topic that must be talked about amongst men more often. Too many are dealing with untold issues caused by hidden pain. When you hide pain inside your heart, it causes other areas of your life to suffer.

As you transition into manhood, it is vital to process hidden pain before pursuing relationships. Suppressed issues that you do not deal with now will resurface at some point. Rejection, bitterness, jealously, abandonment, abuse, and low self-esteem are just a few that can negatively impact your future relationships.

Not dealing with hidden pain can cause you to push people away that genuinely care about your wellbeing. Some cultures frown upon counseling, but I encourage every male to get counseling especially if you have gone through a traumatic experience in your life. Sharing life experiences with trusted mentors and coaches can lead to your healing and growth.

Your Thoughts

You must recognize that you cannot make it through this journey alone. You will need help along the way.

The Importance of Forgiveness
Principle #9

Forgiveness – The action or process of forgiving or being forgiven.

Forgiveness is an essential principle to practice on your journey to manhood. It is important to forgive others as well as forgiving yourself. Forgiving someone who hurt you frees you completely from holding on to that negative experience. Matthew 6:14 (TPT) says, *"And when you pray, make sure you forgive the faults of others so that your Father in heaven will also forgive you."* Unforgiveness and refusing to let go of past hurt and issues does more harm to you than the person you are upset with.

Forgiving people that have hurt us is not always easy. You will know that you have truly forgiven them when the negative emotions and thoughts you normally have about that person are no longer there. It is important to note that forgiveness does not mean allowing the person an opportunity to hurt you again. But to be free and be the best you, you must FORGIVE! Forgiving others allows you to move on with your life so that you can continue to allow God to heal your heart and direct your path.

Focus Scripture:

If you have anything against someone, forgive—only then will your heavenly Father be inclined to also wipe your slate clean of sins. (Mark 11:25 MSG)

Your Thoughts

Dealing with Failure
Principle #10

Failure – An act or instance of failing or proving unsuccessful; lack of success.

Failure is something that everyone will experience at some point in their life. It can be a crushing blow to your ego and self-esteem. Many in our society believe that experiencing failure is the same as *being* a failure and this is not true.

Never allow failure to cause you to give up on your dreams and ambitions. In fact, learn from your failures and work harder. View failing as a steppingstone, not a barrier. This perspective will give you the motivation to keep pushing and the determination to never quit.

I have experienced failure in my life. My dream as a kid was to play sports at the collegiate level but due to poor grades, I was not able to. I learned a valuable lesson about being disciplined in school and in life. You will never know how far you can go if you do not commit to what is required of you.

Failure is often portrayed as this bad thing that you cannot come back from. But a change of perspective will help you see your failure as an opportunity to grow. Learning from your failures will teach you important and valuable lessons so you will not repeat the same thing again. When that kind of knowledge is obtained, it allows you to have a better chance at success. If you allow past failures to consume your thoughts and become the focal point of your life you become stagnant. When you are stagnant in life it hinders your ability to grow and prosper as an individual.

I have learned to view failure differently because every successful person has failed at some point on their journey.

Here are three examples:

Michael Jordan, 6-time NBA Champion, was cut from his high school basketball team before becoming one of the greatest players to ever play the game.

Walt Disney, animator and founding visionary of Disney World, was once fired from his job at a newspaper because he "lacked imagination and had no good ideas."

Mark Cuban, entrepreneur & inventor, failed at almost every job he ever had but his refusal to quit eventually paid off when he acquired billions from the sales of multiple companies. He is an investor on ABC's *Shark Tank* and owns the NBA's Dallas Mavericks.

Focus Scripture:

No matter how many times you trip them up, God-loyal people don't stay down long; Soon they're up on their feet, while the wicked end up flat on their faces. (Proverbs 24:16 MSG)

John Bolden

Your Thoughts

In life your actions will always speak louder than your words.

Identity
Principle #11

Establishing your identity as a man is a fundamental key to manhood. Identity can be defined as your character, beliefs, and values. When you do not know your identity, you are subject to believe a false narrative about yourself. While on your journey, the 3 P's - Provider, Protector, and Priest – are foundational building blocks that will help to cultivate and solidify your identity.

Provider – 1. a person or thing that provides. 2. a person who supports a family or another person.

It is important that you provide for your family. But prior to taking care of a family, you must learn to take care of yourself. Invest in your growth and development by prioritizing your personal hygiene & educating yourself via classes, seminars, and workshops. Focus on taking care of your health, maintaining a budget, and securing an apartment or home. Keep in mind that you do not have to compare yourself to anyone else. It is important to create structure in your life so that you have a foundation for your future.

When you have a family, it is important to build on that foundation with your spouse. Providing for your family can be a heavy load if you are not prepared for it. But it is your responsibility to make sure your family is taken care of. Some ways to prepare for the responsibility are:

18 Principles of Manhood for Young Males

- Following the biblical principle of creating multiple streams of income. It is important to pursue a variety of opportunities to provide for your family. Entrepreneurship must be pursued wisely however it can completely change the trajectory of your family tree.
- Developing a savings plan will be vital for leaving a legacy. Be sure to communicate with your spouse about your family budget so that you are on the same page about your life together.
- Investing in Life Insurance, 401K/403(b), Stock Market investments via your employer and/or personal broker, Cryptocurrency, and Land Ownership.
- Knowing and monitoring your credit scores, credit utilization, and protecting your identity from theft.

Being the Provider is not just monetary. It is essential to demonstrate love. Husbands and fathers set the tone and lead by example. Healthy relationships include affection, communication, quality time, words of affirmation, and support. But let me warn you: failing to provide for your family has consequences. As men, we are the anchors for our families. It is important to give your all.

Protector – a person or thing that protects; defender; guardian.

It is important that you protect your family both naturally and spiritually. Being the protector means you keep everyone in your family safe. You do not run at the first sign of trouble and leave your family behind.

Be mindful that you cannot allow any and everything into your home. Watch who you invite into your space. Never allow anyone or anything to create a negative environment around your family.

It is your job to keep watch. The Bible informs us in Luke 18:1 (KJV) that men should always pray. Prayer is vital in protecting your family spiritually. Your spouse should not be the only one praying. God wants to hear your voice too.

Priest – the spiritual covering for your family.

Christ Jesus set the example for us as men. Discipleship of your family starts with prayer. Praying on behalf of your family is critical. Your family should see and hear you lead prayer inside your home. The Bible in Proverbs 22:6 (KJV) says, "train up a child in the way he should go: and when he is old, he will not depart from it." Studying the Word as a family will set the foundation for your marriage and children. It makes a difference when your children see leadership in the home.

<u>Focus Scripture</u>:

But you are the ones chosen by God, chosen for the high calling of priestly work, chosen to be a holy people, God's instruments to do his work and speak out for him, to tell others of the night-and-day difference he made for you—from nothing to something, from rejected to accepted. (1 Peter 2:9-10 MSG)

Your Thoughts

Be willing to learn something new.

Be teachable.

Be Teachable
Principle #12

Teachable – Able to learn by being taught; willing to learn.

Let us first start off by acknowledging this truth...YOU DON'T KNOW EVERYTHING THERE IS TO KNOW IN LIFE! I have worked with hundreds of young males in my career and many were unteachable with horrible attitudes. For some, their negative mindset and opposition to instruction resulted in incarceration. Sadly, many of them went through harsh life experiences like prison before they were ready and willing to listen.

You as a young male must have a humble heart. It is important to recognize that there are older, wiser, and more experienced people around you than your peers. You can avoid mistakes, pitfalls, and bad choices simply by listening to people that share their stories of success and failure.

When you are teachable and have a willingness to learn you will gain an abundance of knowledge and wisdom along the way. When people know that you are willing to receive, it is easier for them to pour out wisdom. Even if you are already familiar with the information that is being shared, listen closely because you never know when you may learn something new. *ALWAYS REMAIN TEACHABLE!*

Focus Scripture:

The wise will hear and increase their learning, And the person of understanding will acquire wise counsel and the

skill [to steer his course wisely and lead others to the truth],
(Proverbs 1:5 AMP)

Your Thoughts

John Bolden

TRUST THE PROCESS.

Accept Correction
Principle #13

Correction – A change that rectifies an error or inaccuracy, the action or process of correcting something or someone.

As young males, being open to correction is necessary. Correction is a part of manhood. You must be open to correction from older and wiser men that can teach you important life lessons. It will not always feel good. Honestly, it may even hurt your feelings, but it will be beneficial to you in the long run.

Proverbs 10:17 (CEV) says, *"Accept correction and you will find life; reject correction, and you will miss the road."* Accepting correction helps you to grow. If no one brings the behavioral dysfunction to your attention, how can you create the change in your life that will prepare you for manhood?

Correction, when given with love, is meant to steer you in the right direction. When someone cares about you, they should tell you the truth. Pay attention to the relationships in your life. Do you trust that the people around you have your best interest in mind?

Do not get defensive. It is crucial that you listen and ask questions. Examine your behavior and be willing to adjust. No one is *always* right. Proverbs 15:5 (MSG) tell us that welcoming correction is a mark of good sense.

***Focus Scripture*:**

Take good counsel and accept correction— that's the way to live wisely and well. (Proverbs 19:20 MSG)

Your Thoughts

John Bolden

Evil Communication
corrupts good manners.

Accountability
Principle #14

Accountability – subject to giving an account; an obligation or willingness to accept responsibility or to account for one's actions.

Surrounding yourself with men that will hold you accountable is a sign of maturity. You cannot do it all on your own. Proverbs 27:17 (NIV) says, *"as iron sharpens iron, so one person sharpens another."* As a young male, the *Me, Myself, and I* mentality can be dangerous. It can lead to isolation and stagnation. Having men in your life that can hold you accountable is necessary for growth and development.

It can seem annoying at first but eventually you will appreciate having people in your life that help you stay focused and on the right path. Accountability can help you gain insight into what is needed to get to the next stage of your life. You do not get that level of guidance from your peers. You need people in your life that are beyond where you are currently to teach you and guide you along the journey. Stay focused.

Focus Scripture:

As iron sharpens iron, so one person sharpens another.
(Proverbs 27:17 NIV)

John Bolden

Your Thoughts

Life is not a guessing game;

you need a plan!

The Importance of Good Character
Principle #15

Your character is the *real* you – it is who you are, your values, and how you conduct yourself in life. There are two aspects of character that I would like to focus on in this chapter and they are trustworthiness and integrity.

Trustworthiness – the ability to be relied on as honest or truthful.

Integrity – The quality of being honest and having strong moral principles; moral uprightness.

Being trustworthy is so vital in cultivating your manhood. Trustworthiness will carry over to school, work, family, business, church and even your relationship with God. When you are known as an honest and trustworthy man, it can open the door to favor and opportunities.

Integrity goes hand in hand with being trustworthy. Integrity can be defined as who you are when no one is looking. Putting on a good act in front of people is easy but good and consistent character is what counts. Friendship, marriage, employment, and even business relationships thrive when you have integrity.

Always remember that whatever has access to your heart will eventually come out in your actions. For example, if you are listening to music that promotes lying, stealing, cheating, lust, profanity, drugs, or promiscuous sex, then you are allowing those words and their attributes to have access to your heart. And when those negative attributes become rooted in your heart, they can become a part of your lifestyle.

"Watch your thoughts, they become your words; watch your words, they become your actions; watch your actions, they become your habits; watch your habits, they become your character; watch your character, it becomes your destiny." – Lao Tzu, Philosopher

Focus Scriptures:

Love and truth form a good leader; sound leadership is founded on loving integrity. (Proverbs 20:28 MSG)

Whoever can be trusted with very little can also be trusted with much, and whoever is dishonest with very little will also be dishonest with much. So if you have not been trustworthy in handling worldly wealth, who will trust you with true riches? (Luke 16:10-11 NIV)

Your Thoughts

Today's decisions manifest tomorrow. So, make decisions you will not regret.

John Bolden

The Role of a Father
Principle #16

I am a husband & proud father of a daughter and son. As my son gets older, I see how he watches me closely and even imitates what he sees me doing. Every day that I validate and encourage him, I can see that he is becoming confident in who he is as a person. His identity is strengthened the more I teach, instruct, and prepare him for his journey into manhood.

Fatherhood can look different for everyone. Sometimes what is seen on TV or in movies is all young men are exposed to. Maybe you know your father and have a great relationship with him. Or maybe you don't have a father present to learn from. Your biological father might be deceased, absent, incarcerated, or a person that you have never known. Or maybe you lack a positive male role model to talk to. It can be frustrating having so many unanswered questions.

The role of a father is to model manhood. Fathers bring love, stability, correction, and guidance to their family and environment. Ultimately, a father's role are the 3 P's discussed in the *Identity* principle. Fathers are Providers, Protectors of their family, and the Priest of their homes.

Focus Scripture:

But you, God, see the trouble of the afflicted; you consider their grief and take it in hand. The victims commit themselves to you; you are the helper of the fatherless. (Psalm 10:14 NIV)

Your Thoughts

Do not become another statistic, instead become a success.

Keep Growing
Principle #17

Personal growth and development are essential as you mature and pursue success in different stages of life. As a young male, it is important to think beyond where you are right now. High school and/or college is not the end of your learning phase. What do you see in your future?

College might not be for you, but success is for you if you are willing to put in the work. Your path to success may include vocational school, launching a business, or landing your dream job. Regardless of where life takes you, you must keep growing.

Guidance provided by an experienced mentor can change your perspective. The right mentor at the right time for the right opportunity can be life changing. Mentors and coaches can help you navigate through challenging seasons of your life so that you do not get stuck or frustrated and quit. Trusted advisors can help you make wise decisions so that you avoid unnecessary mistakes.

Be Teachable throughout your life by reading and listening to books and podcasts that focus on your growth as a man. Blogs, online classes, and friends that are focused on personal development can all ensure you do not become stagnant.

***Focus Scriptures*:**

But grow in the grace and knowledge of our Lord and Savior Jesus Christ. To him be the glory both now and to the day of eternity. Amen. (2 Peter 3:18 ESV)

Your Thoughts

John Bolden

The friends you have now will shape who you are in the future.

18 Principles of Manhood for Young Males

Build A Relationship with God
Principle #18

Having a strong spiritual foundation in Jesus Christ is important. Simply put, building a relationship with God is the most important principle there is for you to master. I decided to make this the last principle because your relationship with God helps to cultivate, sharpen, and enhance all the other principles. Your relationship with God will give you wisdom and instruction to avoid a lot of headaches and pain. Now, this does not mean that you will not experience any problems or pressure as life goes on, but God promised that He will be with you every step of the way.

You may be reading this and having trouble connecting with God because of the lack of a father or positive role models in your life. Not receiving love, direction, or instruction from a father figure can hinder the communication and relationship with our Heavenly Father. In Matthew 6:9 (AMP) Jesus taught the disciples to pray this way, *"Our Father who is in heaven…"*. God desires to communicate with you as Father. Communication is key! It is a pillar to building trust.

We can communicate with Him because of Jesus' sacrifice. Would you be willing to die for someone you love? How does that question make you feel? Jesus Christ gave His life for us so that we can have a chance at eternal life. If you do not know Him already, say this prayer with me:

God, I know I am not where I need to be, but I see that I cannot do this without you. So, God I give you all of me. Romans 10:9 (NIV) says, *"If you declare with your mouth, "Jesus is Lord," and believe in your heart that God raised him from the dead, you will be saved."* So, today I make this confession that Jesus is Lord of my life. Lead me and guide me through the power of the Holy Spirit in this journey of manhood. In Jesus' name. Amen.

2 Corinthians 5:17 (NIV) says, *"Therefore, if anyone is in Christ, the new creation has come: The old has gone, the new is here!"* Congratulations on a fresh new start! Here some ways you can start building a relationship with God:

1. Read the Bible – learning God's Word by studying the Bible and other books (*like this one*).

2. Prayer – daily communication with God strengthens your trust and reliance on Him.

3. Find a local church – joining a Christian community and walking with other men of faith will help you grow.

4. Worship – living a lifestyle of honesty and devotion to God so that your life matches your belief.

5. Ask Questions – seeking out guidance and wisdom from God and teachers, coaches, and mentors.

Focus Scripture:

But you will receive power when the Holy Spirit comes on you; and you will be my witnesses in Jerusalem, and in all

Judea and Samaria, and to the ends of the earth. (Acts 1:8 NIV)

John Bolden

Your Thoughts

The journey to manhood requires transparency and guidance.

PRAYERS

God, I forgive everyone that has hurt me from my childhood. I will no longer hold a grudge against them. I release the anger that I had toward them and will no longer hold them in unforgiveness for what happened in the past. Thank you for showing me an example of selfless love by laying your life down for me. Today, Lord, I choose to love those that have hurt me in the past. 1 Peter 4:8 (NIV) says, *"love each other deeply, because love covers over a multitude of sins."* Thank you, God, for the strength and ability to forgive and release all anger and hatred from my heart. In Jesus' name. Amen.

Lord God, I thank you for creating me to be a man that will serve you with my whole heart. I will trust you even when my situation seems difficult to face. Proverbs 3:5-6 (NIV) says, *"Trust in the Lord with all your heart and lean not on your own understanding; in all your ways submit to him, and he will make your paths straight."* So, Lord, I give you my heart, and I put all my trust in You. I may not always understand everything as I walk with you, but I am willing to go through this journey with you Lord. In Jesus' name. Amen.

18 Principles of Manhood for Young Males

www.ingramcontent.com/pod-product-compliance
Lightning Source LLC
Chambersburg PA
CBHW050445010526
44118CB00013B/1682